Scrooby ★

HOLLAND

ENGLAND ★ Amsterdam
★ Leyden

★ Southampton

THE MAYFLOWER

OCEAN

The PILGRIMS' VOYAGE to AMERICA

★ **Scrooby**—where Separatist Pilgrims lived in England
★ **Amsterdam and Leyden**—where Separatists lived in Holland
★ **Southampton**—where Pilgrims boarded the Mayflower
★ **Jamestown**—the first English town in America
★ **Provincetown**—where the Pilgrims first landed in America
★ **Plymouth**—the Pilgrims' home in America

BOOK CLUB EDITION

Meet the
PILGRIM
FATHERS

By ELIZABETH PAYNE

Illustrated by H. B. VESTAL

Step-Up Books   Random House
New York

Contents

1 Secret Meetings 3

2 The Separatists in Holland 6

3 Strangers on the Mayflower 13

4 False Starts to a New Land 17

5 Farewell to the Known 20

6 Troubles at Sea 25

7 Laws for the Wilderness 30

8 Look Out for Indians 35

9 Indians Are Sighted 41

10 Indians Attack 45

11 A Home at Last! 51

12 Fire! Fire! 55

13 An Indian Comes to Plymouth 58

14 Friends or Enemies? 64

15 Alone With the Indians 69

16 A Great Leader Dies 73

17 Trading Beads for Furs 77

18 A Time for Thanks-Giving 80

19 The Pilgrims' Historian 84

1
Secret Meetings

In the year 1606 a group of people called Separatists were living in Scrooby, England.

On Sundays the Separatists met secretly in each other's houses. They met to worship God. Their meetings were against the law. The law said Englishmen could meet to worship God only in King James's churches. King James made all the religious rules for his churches.

The Separatists would not obey the King's religious rules. They felt they must live by the rules of the Bible. They chose their own church leader. And they met with him secretly. This made the King very angry. He said no one could have a church separate from his.

He had the Separatist leaders put in jail. But as soon as they were let out, the Separatists began to hold their meetings again. King James got angrier and angrier. He sent men to spy on the Separatists and break up their meetings. At last the Separatists could stand it no longer. They decided to leave England and go to Holland.

There was a law that no one could leave England without the King's permission. The Separatists knew the King would never give them permission to leave England. But that did not stop the Separatists.

One by one they sold their little houses and farms. By twos and by threes they went secretly to the sea coast. They hired boats. They sailed across the English Channel.

By the end of 1608 about 125 of the Separatists had escaped to Holland. There was no king in Holland. In Holland people could worship as they pleased.

2
The Separatists in Holland

The Separatists were happy in Holland. No one spied on them. They were free to meet whenever they wanted. Most wonderful of all, they could have their very own church.

Sometimes the Separatists longed for the English farms they had sold. Sometimes they worried that they all had to work hard for very little money. But their religion meant everything to them. It meant more than money. It meant more than living in England. It even meant more than having their children grow up to be more like Hollanders than Englishmen.

The Separatists lived in Holland for 11 years. Then there was talk that Spain was going to declare war on Holland. The Separatists knew the king of Spain was a Catholic. If the Spanish king ruled Holland, the Separatists knew their church would be closed.

A Separatist leader named William Brewster suggested they all leave Holland before war came. But where could they go? All of Europe except Holland was ruled by kings with strong feelings about religion.

William Brewster said he knew of a place where people might worship as they pleased. That place was called America.

Separatists feared the very name America. America was a wild and dangerous land. It belonged to the Indians. There was nothing there. There were no houses. There were no stores. There were no towns.

There was one English town in America, Brewster said. It was called Jamestown. Jamestown had been built and settled by people who had been sent to America by English business men. The people in Jamestown had a hard time at first. But they had survived.

Brewster was sure the Separatists could survive in America, too. And perhaps they could even get some business men to send them there.

Finally, about 100 Separatists said they would go to America if a way to get there could be found. They found some English business men who became their partners. The business men hired a ship called the Mayflower. They also bought some of the food and supplies the Separatists would need in America.

For their part, the Separatists agreed to work in America for seven years. They would cut wood and get furs for the business men to sell in other parts of the world. After seven years the partners would divide the money that had been made. Then the Separatists would be free to work for themselves.

When it came time to sign the partnership papers, some of the Separatists changed their minds. Finally, the Separatists had to tell the business men that only 47 of them were going. Separatists John Carver and William Brewster were afraid the business men would call off the trip. Both Brewster and Carver hurried to see the business men.

But the business men had found 70 people who wanted to work in America. By twos and threes these people were coming to Southampton, England, where the Mayflower was waiting to sail.

3
Strangers on the Mayflower

Soon the Southampton dock was filled with people the business men had found. Some, like William Mullins and John Billington, had brought their families. Others, like the young barrel-maker John Alden, had come alone.

These people were not going to America for religious reasons. Most of them were going because they could not find work in England. They brought the little they owned with them. Many of them were sure they would never see England again.

The Mayflower's sailors made fun of the passengers. The passengers paid no attention. They were far too busy. They were carrying tools and cooking pans and bedding on board. They were also trying to get a fishing boat onto the ship. At last they sawed it into four pieces. Only then could they find room for it on the Mayflower.

One of the Mayflower's passengers was trying to keep out of sight. He was the Separatist leader, William Brewster. King James's men wanted to arrest him. So Brewster had to hide until the Mayflower sailed. But it could not sail until the other Separatists got to Southampton.

Young William Bradford had written from Holland to say they were on their way.

Days went by. Brewster hoped nothing had happened to Bradford and the other Separatists.

At last they arrived. Their trip had been rough. They had come to England on a small ship called the Speedwell. It was much smaller than the Mayflower. But it was their very own. They had sold their homes to buy it. Bradford and some of the other Separatists planned to sail the Speedwell across the sea right beside the Mayflower. Then they would have their own small ship in America.

4

False Starts to a New Land

The Speedwell tied up beside the Mayflower. The Separatists were glad to see William Brewster and to find out that he was safe. William Bradford was especially glad. For Brewster was like a father to him.

All the Separatists met Captain Christopher Jones of the Mayflower. Captain Jones introduced them to the other passengers who were going to America on his ship.

The Separatists learned that some of these passengers were going to America for adventure.

One of the adventurers was a short man with bright red hair. His name was Myles Standish, and he was a soldier. He brought guns and gun powder onto the Mayflower. He would use them to protect the settlers from Indians in America.

The Separatists made friends with Myles Standish and all the others. Everyone helped the Separatists get the Speedwell ready to sail.

Finally, their boat was ready.

Twice the two ships started out. Twice they turned back because the Speedwell was leaking. At last it was decided the Speedwell could not be fixed. This meant that the settlers would not have their own little ship in America. It also meant everyone had to go on the Mayflower. But there was not room for 117 people on the Mayflower.

Some were happy to stay behind. They said if all went well they would come to America later.

5
Farewell to the Known

On the morning of September 6, 1620, a fine wind was blowing. There were 102 passengers crowded onto the Mayflower. Captain Jones called to his sailors. Up went the ship's sails. The Mayflower started out to sea. Now all the passengers had one thing in common.

They were all leaving their homes to go to a far-off land. In this way they were all Pilgrims.

The Pilgrims stood together on the ship's deck. They watched the green hills of England slowly drop out of sight. Now the Mayflower was the only home these 102 brave Pilgrims had.

Soon the Mayflower was far out at sea. The Pilgrims turned from the railings. They began to set their home to rights.

The women looked for places for their families to sleep. The only covered deck was very small. There were not enough bunks for everyone. The women put up as many hammocks as they could. Then they made beds on the floor for the rest of the people.

The children explored the ship. They had been told to stay out of the sailors' way. Most of them did. But not the Billington boys. Little Francis and John Billington got into everyone's way.

It was not easy to get away from the Billington boys. The Mayflower was so crowded that no one had a quiet place of his own.

This did not stop the Separatist Pilgrims from having their church meetings. They said their prayers and sang. Often the sailors made fun of the meetings. But, even so, the Separatist Pilgrims met with William Brewster and prayed every morning during the trip.

6
Troubles at Sea

Many of the Pilgrims had never gone so far out to sea before. The rolling of the boat made many of them sick. So did some of the food.

The women had to cook out on the open deck. They could not cook every day. Sometimes the wind blew too hard. Captain Jones was afraid the women's fires might spread and burn up his ship. So on windy days the Pilgrims had nothing to eat but cold, dry food.

For a month the Mayflower had good weather. By early October they were halfway across the sea. Then the ship ran into a storm. Great waves began to crash over the deck. The Captain ordered the sails taken down. He sent all the Pilgrims to the covered deck.

The Mayflower was tossed this way and that. Water ran through the ship. It soaked the Pilgrims' beds. It soaked their food. It soaked their clothes. The Pilgrims were ice-cold and wet to the skin. Many were sick. Many were afraid. The ship creaked and cracked. The Pilgrims were sure the Mayflower was going to break in two.

The Pilgrims huddled together on the covered deck. One day John Howland could stand it no more. He said he had to have some fresh air. John climbed up to the open deck. A great wave rolled the ship to one side. John could not hold on. He fell into the sea.

A rope was hanging over the side of the ship. John grabbed it. He hung on. The sailors pulled him back on board.

The Separatists gave thanks to God that John's life had been saved. A few days later they gave thanks again. As the storm roared outside, Mrs. Stephen Hopkins gave birth to a fine baby boy. She named her son Oceanus because he had been born far out in the Atlantic Ocean.

The ship was in storms most of October. Then the sun came out. The sea grew quiet. The Pilgrims could come up on the open deck again. The cold, fresh November air smelled wonderful to them. But the Pilgrims were thin and weak. They had been at sea for more than two months. They longed for the sight of land.

Just a few days later one of the sailors cried out. He said that he saw Cape Cod ahead. The Pilgrims ran to the Mayflower's railings. In the early morning light they saw a white sand beach. They saw woods and bushes. They saw America.

Captain Jones said that Cape Cod was a long arm of land. It curved out into the sea from a part of America called New England. The Captain said English fishermen and explorers had been to this part of America. But no English people had ever tried to live here. Except for Indians, Captain Jones said, the Pilgrims would have Cape Cod to themselves.

7
Laws for the Wilderness

The Mayflower came to rest in a quiet bay now called Provincetown Harbor. The Pilgrims looked at the land where they would live. Far in the distance they saw a wide river. On the nearby shore the woods came right down to the sea. The skies were filled with birds. And the sea was alive with fish.

The women could not wait to go ashore. But the men were not ready yet. They were busy. They were signing an agreement they had made the night before.

The men had talked late into the night. They had said they were coming to a land that had no laws. They had decided they must make laws of their own. The Separatists had their church laws. The other Pilgrims had none. The Separatists had a leader to see that their laws were obeyed. The other Pilgrims did not have a leader. At last the men had agreed on laws that would be good for all the Pilgrims. Then they had picked Separatist John Carver to be everyone's leader. He would be called governor. He would see that the new laws were obeyed. After the men signed the agreement, they said everyone could go ashore.

But Myles Standish said they could not. He said that he would go ashore first to make sure it was safe. The Pilgrims did not argue with Mr. Standish. He had a quick temper. When he grew angry, his face got as red as his hair.

Myles Standish picked out William Bradford and 13 other men to go ashore with him. He gave each man a gun. Standish said he wanted to make friends with the Indians. But if the Indians shot arrows at them, they were to shoot back.

At the word Indians the women shivered. They prayed that the Indians would be friendly.

8
Look Out for Indians

Standish and the men lowered the Mayflower's rowboat into the water. The Pilgrims on the ship lost sight of the men.

They watched and waited. They heard nothing but the wind and the wild crying of water birds. They saw nothing but gray skies and a cold and lonely land. The afternoon went by. Then, just as it grew dark, the men came out of the woods. They rowed back to the Mayflower.

The men had lots of news. The land seemed good for farming. The trees were fine for building houses and barns. And they had seen no Indians. So it seemed safe for the Pilgrims to go ashore the next day.

But there was bad news, too. All of the water in the ponds was sea water. It was salty. Salt water was no good for drinking or cooking or farming. Unless a fresh-water lake or river was found, the Pilgrims could never settle here.

Standish said as soon as the fishing boat was put together, they would explore farther. The river they had seen in the distance might be a fresh-water river.

But no one went ashore the next day. It was Sunday. The Separatist Pilgrims spent the day praying.

On Monday the men brought the four pieces of the fishing boat up from the Mayflower's hold. Piece by piece the sailors took it ashore. Then the sailors rowed Standish and some of the men to the beach. Standish told the men to stand guard near the woods. No one had seen a sign of an Indian. But Mr. Standish was taking no chances.

Standish told the sailors to bring the carpenters to shore next. He wanted them to get right to work nailing the fishing boat together again.

After a while all the Pilgrims were ashore. The women washed the family clothes. The children raced up and down the sand. Before long the women and children were wet and cold. But it felt wonderful to be on land again.

As the sun went down, Standish said everyone must get back to the Mayflower. He did not want to meet Indians for the first time in the dark.

Standish was also worried about
something else. The carpenters
had told him it would take days
to fix the fishing boat. He could
not wait days for the boat. Winter
was coming. Before it came, he
must find a place for the Pilgrims
to live. Standish decided to set
out on foot as soon as he could.

9

Indians Are Sighted

Two days later Myles Standish and 15 men set off to look for the river they had seen from the deck of the Mayflower. The men marched down the beach in single file.

They had been marching for about an hour when all at once they saw five Indians. The Indians raced into the woods. Standish led his men into the woods right after them. He wanted to show the Indians that the Pilgrims were not afraid of them. But the Indians had vanished.

The Pilgrims pushed on through the woods toward the river.

The men struggled along for two days. They had the feeling that Indians were hiding behind every tree. But they saw no one. At last they came to the river. They found it was not a river at all. It was salt water that came from the sea.

The discouraged men went back to the Mayflower. There was a meeting to decide what to do.

Their fishing boat was fixed now. They could use it to go exploring. But the Mayflower sailors did not want to wait until the Pilgrims found a home. They wanted to sail back to England. But Captain Jones said he would not go until the Pilgrims were settled.

That was good to hear. But the Pilgrims knew the Mayflower could not stay with them forever. They asked Captain Jones if there was any place else they could go. The Captain got out his maps. One of his officers, named Robert Coppin, pointed out a place called Plymouth.

Coppin said that he had been to Plymouth once. It had fresh water and a fine harbor. If the land was good for farming, it might be just the place for the Pilgrims.

Plymouth was 45 miles away. Mr. Standish said he and some of the men would go there at once in the fishing boat. Coppin said he would go along to show them the way.

10

Indians Attack

The day was cold and windy when the men set out. It began to rain. Then it snowed. High waves rocked the little fishing boat. The men's clothes were soaked with ice-cold water. Their wet clothes froze in the cold, cold air. But the men sailed on all day. When it grew dark they took their boat to shore. They made a fire on the beach. They cut down branches and put them all around the fire.

The men hoped that the branches would keep out the cold wind. They also hoped the branches would keep out any Indian arrows that might come their way.

No arrows came their way the first night. But the second night they were glad they had branches around them. Just before dawn the Pilgrims heard wild cries in the woods. A shower of arrows whistled through the air.

The Pilgrims ran for their guns. The wild cries grew louder. The arrows came faster. The Pilgrims could not see the Indians. But they sent shot after shot into the woods. Then they saw one Indian hiding behind a tree. The Pilgrims shot at him. The shots missed. The Indian gave a yell and ran into the woods. Then all of the cries and arrows suddenly stopped.

Standish ordered the Pilgrims to follow the Indians. But once again the Indians had vanished. Standish called off the hunt. They could not take time to chase Indians this day. They had to find Plymouth.

The men sailed on through rain and snow. The waves almost turned the boat over. The men hung on tight. As night fell, Robert Coppin saw Plymouth ahead. A large wave carried the boat up onto the shore. The men could not see where they were or if Indians were about.

The Pilgrims were afraid. Their guns were wet, and wet guns would not fire. They stayed close to their boat all night.

When morning came, the men saw they were on a small island about three miles from Plymouth. They decided to wait where they were until their guns were dry. They had to wait two days. It was Monday when the Pilgrims went ashore.

Everything about Plymouth made them happy. William Bradford said it was "a most hopeful place." The land was good for planting. There were two fine rivers. The harbor was deep enough for a ship as big as the Mayflower. And they saw no Indians. The men sailed back to the Mayflower with their good news.

At last they had found a place in America for the Pilgrims to live.

11
A Home at Last!

On Saturday, December 16, 1620, the Mayflower came to rest in the harbor at Plymouth. Many of the Pilgrims lay sick in bed with high fevers. The Pilgrims had not had fresh vegetables or fruit for four months. This bad diet had made many of them ill. The Pilgrims who were well did all they could for their sick friends. Even so, six Pilgrims never saw their new home. They were dead before the end of December.

The Pilgrims buried their dead. But they had no time to sit and mourn. They had to start building their town as fast as they could.

The men worked in rain and snow and sleet. They cut down trees. They sawed them into boards. Each night they took their tools back to the Mayflower. They were afraid Indians might steal them.

Everyone knew there were Indians near by. They had seen smoke from Indian fires. Standish said it would save time to leave the tools on shore. He said 20 men should take turns guarding them. The 20 men cut down branches. They made huts of the branches to sleep in.

It was cold and windy. Everyone caught colds, but they kept working. First they worked on their meeting house. Many people would be able to sleep in it while the 19 small family houses were being built.

When the walls of the meeting house were up, the men moved into it. They lit a fire on the dirt floor. They slept in their clothes. Still they were cold. Many men got too sick to work. Those who could work started to build houses for their families. In a month's time a few family houses had been built. But the work went slowly. Everyone was hungry and weak.

12
Fire! Fire!

Before January was half over, the
meeting house was full of sick men.
They lay on the dirt floor around a
fire. One morning a spark flew up
from the fire. The next minute the
meeting house roof was in flames.
The men stumbled out into the cold.
Sick as they were, they ran back
and forth between the shore and
the meeting house with buckets of
water. Somehow they managed to
put out the roof fire before the
building burned.

The Pilgrims had trouble after trouble. They had trouble fishing. Their fish hooks were the wrong size. They had trouble hunting, too. Their guns were not made to fire quickly. Birds and deer often got away before the men could fire a shot. So most days the hunters came home without food for their families to eat. Before the end of January, eight Pilgrims died of hunger and colds. And more and more people were sick.

One day in February a Pilgrim was in the woods trying to shoot wild duck. All at once he saw 12 painted Indians creeping toward Plymouth. He ran to tell Standish.

On the way he met Pilgrims who were cutting down trees in the woods. They dropped their axes and ran to town, too. Standish ordered the men to stand ready with their guns. The Pilgrims waited. Hours went by. Not an Indian was seen. But the Indians had been close by. When the men went back to work, their axes were gone. Sick or well, some men would have to watch for Indians all night from now on.

By the end of February another 17 Pilgrims had died. Standish said the dead must be buried at night. He said the Indians were sure to attack if they knew that only 71 Pilgrims were still alive.

13
An Indian Comes to Plymouth

Standish was worried. Indians might attack from anywhere. The tired and sick Pilgrim men could not stand watch all the time. They had to finish their houses.

With the help of Captain Jones,
Standish brought big guns ashore
from the Mayflower. He placed
them on a hill. Some guns pointed
at the sea. Some pointed at the
woods. A few men behind the guns
could now protect the Pilgrims
from Indians.

Days went by. The Pilgrims were worried about Indians. But they worried even more about sickness. Every week more Pilgrims died. Yet the men kept on working in the cold March wind. They had planned to build 19 family houses. Now they would not need that many.

As the houses were finished, the men and women raked their land to get it ready for planting. They were sure Indians were all around. But no Indians attacked.

Then on the morning of March 16, the village was terrified. Out of the woods stepped a tall, straight-backed Indian. The men ran toward him. He marched right up to them.

"Welcome," the Indian said. Then he smiled a great big smile. He said his name was Samoset and that he would like to be friends.

The Pilgrims could not believe their ears. A friendly Indian who spoke English was the last thing they had expected. Samoset told them he had met Englishmen before. English fishermen had come to the shores near his home. He said the fishermen had been friendly. They had taught him English. They had given him beer. The Pilgrims had no beer. But they made Samoset as welcome as they could. They gave him some dry cheese and a little piece of duck to eat.

Samoset told the Pilgrims that Plymouth had once belonged to an Indian tribe. All the tribe died of a sickness except one man. His name was Squanto. Squanto had been captured by a sea captain and taken to Spain. Squanto escaped. He went to England. There he made friends with a man who taught him English. Later the man sent Squanto back to America on a fishing boat.

Indians from another tribe had been captured with Squanto. But they had never been seen again. So their tribe, the Nausets, hated all white men. Samoset said it was the Nausets who had attacked the Pilgrims on Cape Cod. It was the Nausets who had stolen the axes of the Pilgrims. It was the Nausets who were hiding around Plymouth right now.

Samoset said he knew the Nausets' chief. His name was Massasoit. Chief Massasoit ruled all the tribes for miles around. Samoset said he would go to see Chief Massasoit. He was sure the chief would get back the Pilgrims' axes for them.

14

Friends or Enemies?

Samoset did as he said he would do. In two days he was back with the Pilgrims' axes. A few days later he came back again. This time he brought Squanto with him.

Squanto spoke English better than Samoset. Squanto told the Pilgrims how glad he was to meet them.

As Squanto was talking to the Pilgrims, 60 Indians led by Chief Massasoit stepped out of the woods.

The Pilgrims felt they had been tricked. They were sure the Indians had come to kill them.

Samoset saw the Pilgrims were afraid. He said Chief Massasoit wanted to be friends, too. Squanto said Massasoit was a very important man. He had made the Nausets give back the Pilgrims' axes. Squanto said that an Indian chief should be treated as if he were a king.

The Pilgrims ran to get a small green rug and some pillows. These were the prettiest things they had. They spread out the rug for the Chief to sit on. Then Governor Carver greeted Massasoit as he would have greeted a king. Carver bowed low and kissed the Chief's hand. Massasoit kissed Carver's hand right back.

Then Massasoit began to talk. Squanto told the Pilgrims what he said. Massasoit said that his people would never hurt the Pilgrims. He said they would put down their bows and arrows whenever they met a Pilgrim. And they would never take the Pilgrims' tools again.

For these kind things Massasoit wanted something in return. He asked the Pilgrims to be on his side if there was an Indian war. He was sure he could win any war with the Pilgrims' terrible guns.

The Pilgrims thought Massasoit was asking very little and offering a lot. They said they would be glad to be Massasoit's friend and ally.

15

Alone With the Indians

At first the Pilgrims could not really believe the Indians wanted to be friends. But the Indians soon proved it. Squanto came to live with the Pilgrims. He showed them the best places to fish. He showed them the best place to plant corn.

Other Indians moved to the fields near by. Though they were also planting corn, they never touched the Pilgrims' tools. And each time they saw a Pilgrim they put down their bows and arrows.

Brewster said the Pilgrims should give thanks to God for sending them friendly Indians. He said he was sure everything would be better now. But in March more Pilgrims died. By the first of April only 51 were left, and almost half of them were children. Only 20 men and 8 women had lived through the awful winter. So only seven houses would be needed. Sadly, Brewster and Bradford and Standish helped the other men finish the town.

The last people moved from the Mayflower to shore. They came with boxes of beads and knives. They would need these things to buy furs from the Indians.

Squanto was sure the Indians would trade their furs for beads and knives. The business men had asked that furs be sent back on the Mayflower. But Captain Jones said his sailors would not wait for the Pilgrims to make any trades. He said the business men would have to send another ship for the furs.

On April the fifth, the Mayflower sailed away. The little group of Pilgrims watched the ship sail slowly out to sea. In their hearts some of them may have wished they were sailing for England, too. But not one Pilgrim had asked to go.

16
A Great Leader Dies

The Pilgrims settled down in their small houses. The children whose mothers and fathers had died moved in with other families. Many of the Indians almost became part of the Pilgrims' families, too. They kept dropping in at meal time. They all loved the Pilgrims' food.

The women were glad to have good Indian friends. But they wished their new friends would not come to dinner quite so often. There were fewer Pilgrims to feed now, but food was still scarce.

Food would have been even scarcer without Squanto. He caught eels and lobsters for the Pilgrims to eat. He brought them little fish to put in the soil. He buried the fish in the ground with the corn seeds. He said the fish were good for the soil. And they were. The corn began to grow.

The men worked in the corn fields every day. One hot day Governor Carver said he did not feel well. The men took him to his house. A few days later he was dead. Now the Pilgrims had no governor. They had no one to see that their laws were kept. They had no one to deal with the Indians for them.

The Pilgrims thought that William Brewster would be a good governor. But Brewster said he would not take the job. He was their church leader. He did not want to mix the church with law.

The Pilgrims then elected William Bradford as governor. He was much younger than Brewster. He was only 31 years old. But he knew how to get things done.

Governor Bradford sent Squanto to Massasoit with a message. The Pilgrims had to get furs from the Indians to send back to England. Bradford asked Massasoit to tell his friends that the Pilgrims would give them beads and knives for furs.

17
Trading Beads for Furs

Soon the Indians began bringing furs into Plymouth. They loved the things the Pilgrims gave them for their furs. They would take all day to choose some pretty beads or a long metal knife. Sometimes the Indians wanted both. So they would hurry off to get more furs. Indians came and went all summer. Soon John Alden had barrels and barrels of furs ready to ship back to the business men.

The Pilgrims wanted still more furs. They wanted to make up to the business men for not sending any back on the Mayflower. The Pilgrims did a lot of trading. Their supply of beads and knives was getting low. But they decided to keep trading as long as they could.

The summer went by, but no ship came. Soon the Pilgrims had all the furs of the Indians who lived near by. So Squanto and Standish went off in the boat to visit other tribes. Squanto said some of these tribes were bad. He told Standish to scare them with his gun and just take their furs. But Standish would not do it.

Standish gave the Indians all the knives and beads he had. When he had finished trading, the Pilgrims had many new Indian friends. They also had many more furs.

As the weeks went by, the Pilgrims made more and more Indian friends. They were no longer afraid to let their children go into the woods alone. Indians helped the children pick baskets of wild fruit. They showed the children where to find nuts. Indians helped the Pilgrim women grind corn into flour. From the flour the women made good hot corn bread. Then the Indians sat down with the Pilgrims and had some.

18
A Time for Thanks-Giving

For the first time since they had come to America, the Pilgrims had all the food they needed.

Their corn had grown strong and tall. Their houses had been made ready for winter. They had piles and piles of wood for their fires.

They had barrels and barrels of furs ready to ship to England.

By October their corn was picked. Governor Bradford said it was a time for thanks-giving.

The Pilgrims invited all of their Indian friends to come to Plymouth. The women made lobster pies. They roasted ducks and turkeys. The children went into the woods to find nuts and berries. Tables were set out under the trees.

Indians came from far and near. Massasoit arrived with 90 men. He brought a present of five large deer. They roasted the deer over big, open fires.

Soon all was ready.

The Pilgrims and Indians ate and ate. They ate and sang and danced for three days. It was a happy time. The Pilgrims gave thanks to God that their lives had been spared. They gave thanks for the food and friends they found in America. Thus, the Pilgrims began a custom of Thanksgiving that still lives on.

The little band of brave Pilgrims would have hard times again. But no time would ever be as hard for them as their first winter in the wilderness. The courage and the strength of this little group of people have become a legend. They are the most famous of the early settlers of America. Today we call them the Pilgrim Fathers.

19
The Pilgrims' Historian

We know most of what we know about the Pilgrims from William Bradford. Bradford was elected governor of Plymouth 30 times. He kept a careful diary.

Bradford tells us that everyone lived by the Pilgrims' laws except John Billington. Billington was hanged for killing a man.

Bradford writes that John Alden and Priscilla Mullins were married.

He tells us that Chief Massasoit stayed friends with the Pilgrims all of his life.

Bradford writes about the ships the business men sent to Plymouth. The Pilgrims sent the ships back full of furs and wood.

On every ship the Pilgrims also sent back glowing letters about America to their friends. These letters brought more and more people across the sea to Plymouth. Soon the town was crowded.

Myles Standish and some of the other people started farms outside the town.

Bradford tells about the other people who came to America from England. Some of these people were Puritans. Like the Separatists, the Puritans left England for religious reasons. Many Puritans settled near the Pilgrims.

The Pilgrims always had to work hard. But they were happy. They had their own churches, and they could live as they pleased. The lives they led showed the rest of the world that people could have religious freedom in America. And in Plymouth Colony, the Pilgrims showed that people could govern themselves very well without a king.

AMERICA

NEW ENGLAND

Plymouth ★
Cape Cod ★
Provincetown

★ Jamestown

THE VOYAGE OF

ATLANTIC